Maria DesJarlait is an indigenous woman who is from the Arikara tribe of Fort Berthold reservation in North Dakota and Ojibwe from Red Lake, Minnesota. She was raised on the reservation in North Dakota and had big city dreams. She went on to college in Chicago, Il where she earned her bachelor's degree in early childhood education and English as a second language. She is married to her best friend Joel and has two daughters Aiyanna and Ayasha that keep her plenty busy. She teaches Preschool in Illinois where she seen the need for books that represent Native American children as people of today. She wrote this book based on her experiences as a child with her grandmother and her two daughters' experiences with their adventurous grandmother Peggy as well. This is her story that she hopes to inspire more Native American children to dream big. Miigwetch (thank you)!

Maria DesJarlait

Illustrated By: **Negwes White**

AUSTIN MACAULEY PUBLISHERS®

LONDON • CAMBRIDGE • NEW YORK • SHARJAH

Ordering Information
Quantity sales: Special discounts are available on quantity purchases by corporations, associations, and others. For details, contact the publisher at the address below.

Publisher's Cataloging-in-Publication data
DesJarlait, Maria
Who Am I?

ISBN 9798889102250 (Paperback)
ISBN 9798889102274 (ePub e-book)

Library of Congress Control Number: 2024913174

www.austinmacauley.com/us

First Published 2024
Austin Macauley Publishers LLC
40 Wall Street, 33rd Floor, Suite 3302
New York, NY 10005
USA

mail-usa@austinmacauley.com
+1 (646) 5125767

To my husband, daughters and son.

I would like to thank my beloved family and community for inspiring me to create.

I would like to thank my mother for teaching me that courage brings advantage and success and my grandmother for teaching me that gentleness and kindness are the greatest ways to reciprocate.

I would like to thank my husband for his constant love, devotion and support, all of which I wholeheartedly appreciate.

I would like to say Miigwetch/wetAxkoosšteéRAt (thank you) to my late grandmother Peggy M. DesJarlait (big Peggy) and mother Peggy Ann DesJarlait (little Peggy) for giving me and my daughters these teachable moments that are lifelong learning experiences that will continue to be passed down to each generation. My grandmother played such a huge role in my life that helped shape me as a strong indigenous woman with a great appreciation for my culture and its teachings. I would also like to say thank you to the late Fr. Peter Powell of St. Augustine's church who helped my family for four generations. His church and the Native American Indian summer programs had molded me into the teacher and now writer that I am. So many times, I had wanted to discontinue my education and Fr. Powell and his amazing staff counseled me and prayed with me helping me realize that I already had the tools to succeed.

Also, a special note of gratitude to Dr. Logan Sutton of MHA Nation Culture and Language department, Wayne Flute, Thomas Plenty Chief, Dr. Zoe Brown of University of Minnesota Ojibwe and nimishoomis Mike Beaulieu for helping share their vast knowledge of our indigenous language

Lastly, Miigwetch/wetAxkoosšteéRAt (thank you) to all my elders from both of my communities of Fort Berthold reservation in ND and Red Lake reservation in Mn. For the many elders who came to our schools and spoke to us, for my elders who help keep and practice our traditions. Those that remind us to never forget who we are, where we come from and how far we have come.

Ojibwe Glossary

Hello: Boozhoo Bo-zh-oo

My Grandma: Nookomis Nah-ko-mis

My grandpa: Nimishoomis Neh-mish-o-mis

My Mother: Nimaamaa Neh-ma-ma

My aunt (mom's sister): Ninoshenh - Neh-no-shay

My aunt (dad's sister): or Nizigos -Neh-ze-goes

My relative:Indinawemaagan - In-dah-nah-way-mah-ghan

Thank you: Miigwech Me-gw-ech

Men's traditional dancer: Bwaanzhii-niimi Bwa-zhe-nee-mee

Singer: Negamod Nah-gah-ma-nd
Tobacco: Asemaa Ah-see-mah

Bear: Makwa Mah-k-wa

Arikara Glossary

Hello: **nawáh** – nah-wah

Grandma: **atíka'** – ah-dee-gah

Grandpa: **atípa'** – ah-dee-ba

Aunt: **atiná'** – aht-nah : (same as the word for mother)

Sisters / Cousins: **inaáni'** – ee-non-nee :: (this is a sister of a woman; there's a different word for sister of a man)

My sister (or our sister): **atítat** – ah-dee-dot

His sister (or their sister): **itáhni'** – ee-dah-nee

Your sister: **átat** – ah-dot

Grass Dancer: **WIšó'Iš** – hw-shoh-ish

Men's traditional dancer: **hirúškA** – hee-doosh-k

Singer: **naanoókUx** – non-no-kw

Tobacco: **naaWIškaánu'** – now-sh-gone-noo

Bear: **kuúNUx** – goon-nh

Thank you: wetAxkoosšteéRAt – wait-h-go-s-shtare-t or shortened version **goshtay** – go-shtay

Nawáh/Boozhoo! (Hello!) I'm Giovonni, but everyone calls me by my spiritual name *Makwa,* which means 'bear' in my native Ojibwe language. I live in a beautiful place called Fort Berthold Reservation in North Dakota. Right now, I'm visiting *atiná'* (aunt) and *atítat* (sisters) in Chicago, where I joined a basketball camp. It has been so much fun but I miss my home. Right now it's summer, my favorite time of the year, because when I step outside of *aítka's* (grandma) house, I close my eyes and feel the strong warm wind brush across my face, the smell of freshly cut grass and the wind carrying the beats of the drums from across the lake.

Its powwow season, meaning indigenous people like me go to dance and sing. Powwows are competitions to see who the best dancer is, but it is also a place for prayer and to reunite with family and friends. I just like to watch and get the best fry bread there is from *aítka's* food truck. *Atiná'* (aunt) and *atítat* (sisters) dance at the powwows.

Atítat, Aiyanna and Ayasha are coming home with me now that basketball camp is over. Aiyanna is only 9 months older than me, but she thinks she is an adult compared to me. Always nagging at me. Today, she told me, "Why don't you ever dance with me and Ayasha at the powwows?" I just turned around and ignored her.

Did she leave me alone? No! She kept on nagging like she always does, "Makwa… Makwa… Makwa…" Finally, I annoyingly said, "What is it, Aiyanna?" She stared right at me for the longest time and then finally said, "I forgot," and walked away smirking. She does this on purpose to annoy me, I know she does.

The day after we arrived at *atíka's* house, she was preparing her food truck for the powwow that weekend. You know what that means? Yes! It is time for the golden soft pillows that we call fry bread. *Atiná'* and *atítat* are busy at the last minute as usual, trying to sew the rest of their regalia for the powwow. *atítat* dances jingle which is the medicine dress. Ayasha starts to practice her steps before grand entry. She looks at me and says, "Makwa, come dance with us, please?"

I hold my breath for a minute, not knowing what to really say. "Naw, maybe the next one." Ayasha looks at Aiyanna as she shakes her head.

Then, *atiná'* walks by me and whispers in my ear, "Makwa, come dance alongside me, my boy. It will bring good medicine to us since I've been sick for a long time now." I could not say no to that, so I just walked beside her, silently praying that my *atiná'* stays strong and healthy.

The next day, *nookomis* and *nimishoomis* (grandma and grandpa in Ojibwe) drove all the way from their home of Red Lake, Minnesota, for this powwow. I was so happy to see them! *Atiná'* said, "Go for a drive with your grandpa to get some snacks from the store." I jumped in *nimishoomis'* truck and as I was putting on my seat belt, he turned up the radio and had powwow music on. *Nimishoomis* started to sing along and rock his head to the drumbeats.

After a while, he turned down the radio and said "Makwa, who are you?"

I laughed at *nimishoomis* and replied, "Um, I'm Makwa, your favorite grandchild of course!"

Nimishoomis said, "What did you think of when you hear the drums?" I told him that it makes me think of home and of summertime. I really missed that when I was in Chicago. When I was in Chicago and I stepped outside of atiná's house, I could feel the humidity push against my face with the taste of smog in my mouth. I heard the buses, car horns and jack hammers from construction sites all at once. If I were to close my eyes I think I would feel dizzy.

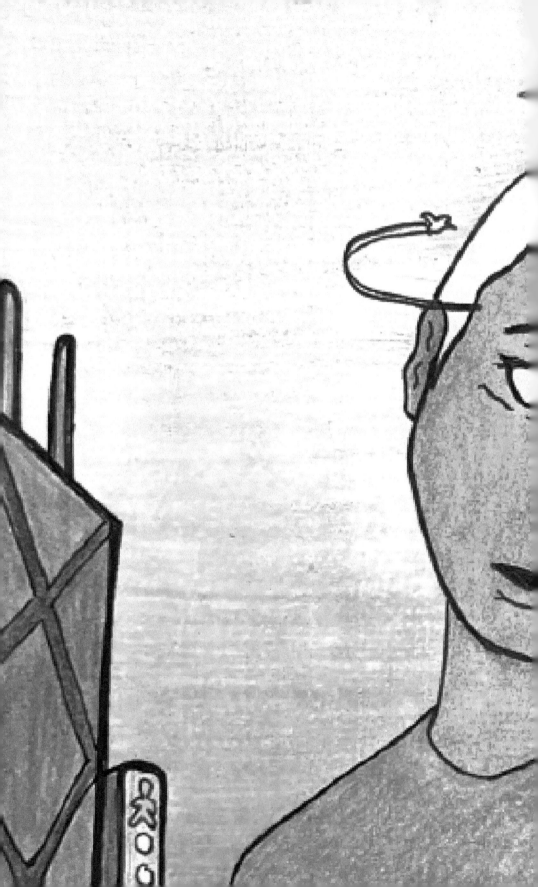

Nimishoomis said, "But what did you hear?" I didn't know what to say. *Nimishoomis* pulled over to a butte called 'Crow flies high' and turned to me and said, "How do you honor our ancestors? How can you help our people and the land?" He told me, "You don't have to answer now, but tell me when it finally comes to you."

"Who am I?"

A grass dancer whose regalia sways in the wind?

No, that's not in my heart.

Arikara WIšó'Iš

"Who am I?"

A traditional dancer whose dance tells stories of war and hunting?

No, that's not in my heart.

Ojibwe (*Bwaanzhii-niimi)/ hirúškA*

"Who am I?"

A fancy dancer who dances really fast, spinning and moving up and down?

No, that's not in my heart.

I thought to myself, "Who am I? I play basketball and video games with my friends. They don't dance at powwows. *Itáhni'* dances with our other girl cousins. How do I walk between worlds like basketball, video games and still honor my ancestors? Life's hard without my dad, I wish my dad was still here to help me. He has been gone for a really long time"

We made it back to the powwow with snacks. We rushed toward the arena hoping no one was sitting in our powwow chairs. I sat down and felt a deep connection with the beat of the drum. The drum represents the heartbeat of mother earth.

I went back to *nimishoomis* and asked, "What should I do? Where do I even start?"

Nimishoomis said, "Let's smudge about it and leave an offering of tobacco (*asemaa*) by a tree for the creator." We did just that.

The next day, *nimishoomis* and I wore our best ribbon shirts that *nookomis* had made for us. I was smiling ear to ear as we went visiting all the people at the powwow.

Nimishoomis saw a young man he hadn't seen in some time. He said, "Negwes, where have you been? I haven't seen you at any powwows for a while."

Negwes said, "I have been so busy with my new job and my twins, but I finally made it back to the circle. I actually came looking for you today."

Nimishoomis looked confused. Negwes continued, saying "I hadn't been making hand drums for a while but the other night, I had a dream of you singing with one of my drums." Negwes handed him the drum with tobacco (*asemaa*), to show respect and honor.

Nimishoomis hugged Negwes and said "*Miigwech.*" (Thank you.) I asked *nimishoomis* what that was all about. nimishoomis said, "I have to pray on that, go check on your **itáhni'** ."

I found Aiyanna singing by the drum. I hadn't seen her do that before. I started to hum while standing next to her. She offered her hand to me and just like that, it felt like there was a spark in my heart. As if all the dancers, drummers and singers were like one. One pulse, one heartbeat, one purpose and all belonging as one.

After the powwow finished, I felt as if my eyes were seeing something new. An awakening!

I went to visit *atiná'* the next day. She wasn't feeling well. I held her weak hand and asked if she needed anything. *Atiná'* said, "My boy, sing for me like you did at the powwow." I started to sing the melodies I remembered. This made my *atiná's* heart so full. She hugged me so tight, with warm tears streaming down her face.

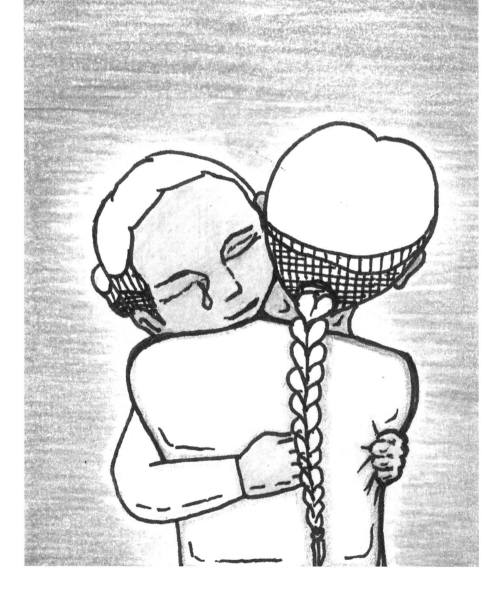

I went to visit *nimishoomis* and told him about *atiná'* being sick. I asked, "How can I help?" *Nimishoomis* went to his room and brought out the hand drum Negwes had given to him, and handed it to me.

Nimishoomis said, "The drum calls for you, you should sing with this drum for healing and honoring. You are a *negamod /naanookUx* (singer.)

I held my hand drum tight and started to beat the drum synced with my heartbeat, and I sang. With each beat of the drum it roared louder inside of me and I squeezed my eyes tight. I thought of my family, my ancestors, *atiná'* and my dad. I asked the creator to guide me. When I opened my eyes I saw my dad smiling at me.

THE END